Care Assistant's
HANDBOOK
The Foundations of Care

By

Ayokanmi Michael

MAPLE PUBLISHERS

Care Assistant's HANDBOOK – The Foundations of Care

Author: Ayokanmi Michael

Copyright © Ayokanmi Michael (2024)

The right of Ayokanmi Michael to be identified as author of this work has been asserted by the author in accordance with section 77 and 78 of the Copyright, Designs and Patents Act 1988.

First Published in 2024

ISBN 978-1-83538-273-8 (Paperback)
      978-1-83538-274-5 (E-Book)

Book cover design and Book layout by:
    White Magic Studios
    www.whitemagicstudios.co.uk

Published by:
    Maple Publishers
    Fairbourne Drive, Atterbury,
    Milton Keynes,
    MK10 9RG, UK
    www.maplepublishers.com

A CIP catalogue record for this title is available from the British Library.

All rights reserved. No part of this book may be reproduced or translated by any form or by any means, electronic or mechanical, including photocopying, recording or by any information storage and retrieval system without written permission from the author.

The book is a work of fiction. Unless otherwise indicated, all the names, characters, places and incidents are either the product of the author's imagination or used in a fictitious manner. Any resemblance to actual people living or dead, events or locales is entirely coincidental, and the Publisher hereby disclaims any responsibility for them.

PREFACE

Discover the essential guide for every care assistant: a comprehensive handbook designed to empower and support those at the forefront of patient care.

This indispensable resource provides clear, practical advice on a wide range of topics, including daily care procedures, effective communication, ethical practices, and self-care strategies. Whether you are a seasoned professional or just beginning your career, this handbook offers the knowledge and confidence you need to excel in your role and make a meaningful impact on the lives of those you care for.

Filled with real-world insights and evidence-based practices, this book is your go-to companion for providing compassionate, competent, and comprehensive care. Embrace the journey of caregiving with the guidance and inspiration found within these pages.

Ayokanmi is a Registered Nurse with over 20 years of experience, she is also a Social Worker and the founder of Ayokanmi Sinmisola Foundation; a nonprofit organization based in Nigeria. She currently works as a Staff Nurse in the UK.

ACKNOWLEDGEMENTS

First and foremost, I would like to express my deepest gratitude to God Almighty for granting me the strength, wisdom, and perseverance to complete this book. Without His guidance and blessings, this work would not have been possible.

To my beloved husband, your unwavering support and encouragement have been my anchor throughout this journey. Your belief in me gave me the confidence to pursue and complete this project.

To my wonderful children, your patience, love and constant support, even when I was preoccupied with writing, have been invaluable. You are my inspiration and my greatest joy.

To all of you, thank you for being my pillars of strength. This book is as much yours as it is mine.

Thank you.

YOUR MOTIVATION

The drive to work in caregiving often stems from a deeply ingrained belief in supporting others. When asked about your motivation, you might not have a specific answer, just a sense that caregiving is your true purpose. For some, caregiving comes naturally from looking after elderly family members, equipping them with essential skills. Others may stumble into it by chance. Regardless of how one enters the field, caregiving is a commendable profession with many rewards. Choosing to be a caregiver is stressful; it means actively engaging with life's complexities, starting early, committing wholeheartedly, and embracing each day fully. It involves appreciating unnoticed moments and providing comfort in overlooked areas. Despite differing motivations, the core of caregiving is a calling to support, heal, and cherish.

As I write my book, a story forms in my mind about a meaningful conversation with a wise elder facing a challenging illness. Her gentle words, spoken through the fog of pain medication, resonated deeply: "You've chosen a less common path, but it is filled with the rarest gems of human connections." These words filled me with renewed vigor. In elderly care facilities, where seniors need extra help, a community of empathetic Carers and Support Workers thrives. The demand for these compassionate individuals is growing, welcoming all who have a passion for caregiving. This manual is a guide for those drawn to or interested in mastering caregiving. With the right tools and self-discovery, anyone can become a compassionate champion, spreading warmth and empathy.

WELCOME TO THE REALM OF COMPASSION

In today's fast-paced healthcare environment, caregivers often go unnoticed despite being true heroes. This guide serves as your reliable companion, leading you through the intricate web of human relationships. Filled with insights and practical advice, it serves as a beacon guiding you towards providing exceptional care. More than just a book, this manual stands as a testament to love, responsibility, and an unwavering commitment to improving lives, uniting all compassionate souls.

QUALITIES OF A CARER

- Understanding and Sensitivity: This involves having empathy, kindness, the ability to understand others' emotions, being aware of their needs, and acting in a way that brings them comfort. Sensitivity is a valuable trait that helps in responding to both people and the environment.

- Willingness to Assist Others: Be attentive and present by listening carefully to those seeking help, making them feel heard, and showing genuine interest in their concerns.

- Capacity for Collaborative Work: Building trust is essential for effective teamwork. Admitting mistakes and finding solutions demonstrates reliability to teammates. Instead of blaming others for errors, show forgiveness, take responsibility, and work together to find solutions.

- Patience and Composure Under Pressure: It is crucial to manage stress, stay productive, enhance organizational skills, adapt to changes, and make well-informed decisions. Embrace constructive criticism, avoid taking things personally, pay attention to details, and perform effectively under pressure.

The importance of effective communication skills when working with elderly people cannot be overstated.

Here are some key tips for enhancing communication in such situations:

- Ensure to maintain eye contact and attentively listen to their needs
- Pay attention to their body language for better understanding
- Promote independence whenever feasible
- Always uphold their dignity and privacy
- Follow their cues and lead in the conversation
- Clearly communicate your intentions
- Stay composed, calm, and patient throughout.

Ayokanmi Michael

This handbook will cover the following areas:
- Direct patient care
- Health observation and documentation
- Safe management of waste
- Hand hygiene
- Appropriate use of PPE
- Safe management of linen
- Building resilience as a caregiver.

DIRECT PATIENT CARE

Direct patient care involves assisting patients with their daily activities that may require specialized knowledge beyond what family members can provide. These tasks are actions done for the patients to make their daily lives more manageable.

Here are the key points about direct patient care:

Supporting residents with their activities of daily living (ADLs) is essential for independent living.

Carers must assist residents with these tasks while upholding their dignity and best interests.

It involves personalizing care, ensuring safety, and maintaining respect throughout the process.

The activities of daily living (ADLs) include:

- Personal hygiene
- Dressing
- Toileting
- Mobility/Transferring/Repositioning
- Nutrition
- Continence
- Environmental hygiene
- Maintaining sleep hygiene

PERSONAL HYGIENE GUIDELINES

- Personal hygiene is a private matter for most individuals, and they prefer to manage it themselves. Some residents find it challenging to allow unfamiliar individuals to assist them, regardless of good intentions. As a caregiver, it is crucial to be patient and respect the residents' autonomy.

  Always seek their consent before providing assistance.

  Clearly explain your intentions and give them ample time to understand and agree.

- When it comes to personal hygiene, many people value their independence. While some may only need gentle reminders, others may require varying levels of assistance - from simple tasks to complete support. Understanding each resident's needs is essential for providing appropriate care. Caregivers must prioritize maintaining the patient's dignity and self-esteem in every task. Encouraging independence is key, supporting residents in tasks they are capable of while intervening only when necessary.

Personal Hygiene Categories:
1. Bathing/Bed bath/washing/showering
2. Shaving
3. Oral care
4. Hair care
5. Nail care

BATHING / BED BATH / SHOWERING

One of the most important things you can do to keep people clean is to help them bath. In addition to removing dirt, sweat, bacteria, and dead skin cells and boosting blood circulation, taking a bath helps the patient feel clean and restore their sense of normalcy.

Keep in mind that assisting people to bath can be a tricky business, as earlier explained, some people are very private and would be reluctant to allow anyone undress them, it is important to introduce yourself and state your role clearly for them, and obtain their consent before attempting to bath for them.

Provide privacy by closing the doors and windows and constantly let them know what you are doing and why you are doing it. This would let them know that you are being considerate of them and not treating them as someone with no input in their own care.

Ask them for their routine as you may want to follow their bathing routine.

Be mindful of the water temperature, not too hot and not too cold, always ask them for their preference and do not make assumptions. Avoid unnecessary exposure, get everything needed ready before the activity.

Watch their mood and be careful not to force them to do what you think is right for them.

Maintain safety at all times by ensuring the floors are not slippery, they are wearing good slippers, using appropriate shower chairs if applicable, that the overhead showers are not loose and swinging, use of bed rails if appropriate etc.

As we grow older, our skin ages and loses fat. It can get dry, brittle, and more prone to damage. To keep skin smooth and supple, you need to apply daily moisturizing cream. Be gentle while applying this because of the fragile nature of their skin.

SHAVING

Shaving may help a person feel better. The frequency with which a person shaves varies depending on their condition and preferences.

Allow the person to shave themselves if possible. You can help by collecting the materials needed and holding the mirror. If you need to do the shaving, ask them if they wish to be shaved in a specific style.

Note that men who have facial hair will require regular shaving, make sure that you note the state of the patient's face and offer them a shave them as required.

Gather the necessary supplies first. You will need to choose between using an electric razor and a regular razor. An electric razor might be the best option for the majority of people.

Compared to a regular razor, electric razors are less likely to result in cuts and nicks. This is particularly crucial if the patient is on blood thinner medications, which can make even small cuts bleed more than usual. Additionally, because there may be more angles on their face to shave, someone who has dropped weight may find it easier to utilize an electric razor.

To ensure that you can both see clearly, make sure the space is well-lit.

ORAL CARE

Maintaining oral hygiene for residents can be a straightforward process.

Encourage patient involvement in the routine. Start by explaining the procedure to the patient and then put on gloves. Place a towel over the patient's chest to keep it dry and elevate their head to a 45-degree angle or higher. Use a toothbrush with a small amount of toothpaste to brush all tooth surfaces.

Moisturize the patient's lips.

Denture Care

Cleaning dentures is essential if the patient wears them. Place a cloth in the sink where dentures will be cleaned to prevent damage if dropped. Replacement of damaged dentures can be costly and affect the patient's ability to eat. With gloves on, remove the patient's dentures and place them in a vomit bowl lined with paper towels. Clean the dentures thoroughly using toothpaste or denture cleanser, rinse them with cool water, and store them in a denture cup with water, denture solution, or mouthwash. Return the dentures to the patient.

Always remove dentures before bedtime to allow the gums to rest and prevent oral health issues.

HAIR CARE

A key component of hygiene is taking care of the hair. It's not necessary to wash a patient's hair every day, but brushing it every day can help keep it from getting tangled. Additionally, brushing will equally disperse oils throughout the hair shaft.

Gently start brushing from the tips of the hair and work your way carefully down to the roots. Hold the hair close to the scalp to avoid pulling excessively if there is a particularly tough area of hair to comb. Applying a tiny bit of petroleum jelly and rubbing it into the tangled hair may be useful if it's an exceptionally tough tangle. Assist the patient in doing the hairstyle they choose. After disinfecting the combing materials, place them back where they belong.

NAIL CARE

Nail care gives the patient a neat appearance and helps prevent them from scratching themselves. Infections can be avoided by regularly cleaning the nails to get rid of microorganisms under the nails. Spend some time examining the patient's fingers, toes, and nails. Take note of and report any foot ulcers, swelling, thick or brittle nails, changes in texture, or colour.

To allow the nails to soften, it is ideal to undertake nail care after taking a bath.

Hand wash before starting any nail care.

Clean the nails. Once the nails are clean, proceed to use nail clippers and trim the nails if necessary. Trim the nail straight and close to the nailbed but leave some room, so you do not cut the patient. Smooth nails with a file if the cut edges are rough.

Rub lotion on the patient's hands.

DRESSING

Dressing means putting on clothes and without having a lot of trouble with standard clothing accessories like buttons or zippers. Along with dressing and undressing, this also entails putting on and taking off all braces, fasteners, and prosthetic limbs as needed.

Making a patient feel comfortable while clothing them is the most important thing for caregivers. The second most important thing is to ask for their preferences and encourage them to dress and undress themselves in order to promote autonomy, only get involved when they are having trouble doing so.

Ensure that you handle the patient with courtesy and avoid undue exposure of their body.

It is crucial to take care not to tug or push them and to make every effort to prevent pain or discomfort. In order to make sure the patient is comfortable, it is advised that you talk with them while dressing them. It is advised to keep clothing within the patients' reach to prevent complications.

Consider the following when dressing for a resident:

- Be mindful of the weather/temperature and activities they will be involved in during the day when helping them to dress up.

- Make decisions simpler. Keep extra clothes out of the closets. Arrange clothes according to the proper order for each item to be worn. Choose something that is easy to wear and basic.
- Choose comfortable shoes.

TOILETING

Helping with toileting is often a crucial aspect of providing care. This could include:

Assisting them to use the toilet when they need to or changing incontinence pads and protecting the health of their skin using emollients or barrier creams.

ASSISTING THEM TO USE THE TOILET

They can more easily empty their bowel and bladder by leaning forward and keeping their feet firmly planted on the ground.

Take your time. It may be necessary for elderly individuals to take their time to ensure that their bladder is empty.

While having a regular schedule might be beneficial, you should also be adaptable and ensure that help is available when needed.

Stick to your scheduled bathroom trips; missing one raises the possibility of an accident.

To improve your comfort level on the toilet, use a soft pillow ring.

Maintain a clutter-free, spotless, and clean bathroom. Also, keep personal hygiene supplies close at hand.

Ensure that the clothing on your resident is simple to put on and take off.

CHANGING PADS

A Carer's daily duties include changing a patient's continence pads; if you know how to do this correctly, the process will go more quickly and easily. Use pads with the appropriate size, kind, and level of absorption to stop leaks.

While changing the pads, staff should ensure that they observe the state of the patient's skin to see if there is redness, or broken skin, these are vital information that should be reported to the nurses. Before using a new incontinence pad, remove the old one, wash the skin with a gentle cleanser, and make sure it's completely dry. Applying barrier cream aids in the prevention of skin issues like infections, rashes, and dryness, it also makes them more comfortable.

For patients who are bed bound, two staff should change their pads because it is unsafe for one staff. This could also cause harm to the skin of the patient.

MOBILITY / TRANSFERRING / REPOSITIONING

Sometimes a patient can have full mobility, limited mobility or no mobility, which means they can either walk with or without aids or they cannot walk at all. A caregiver should always be aware of the patient's mobility status and the degree of assistance needed; these details will be noted in the patient's care plan, which is under the nurses' constant supervision. If a patient uses a walking aid, the caregiver must make sure they always wear appropriate footwear and that the patient is constantly using the aid when walking. It is equally important to note the condition of the aid to be sure that it is in good working order.

For those patients who cannot walk at all, there are means to transfer them to the chair if they are classified as chair bound or even reposition them in bed if they are bed bound.

Encouraging mobility and empowering movement are vital components of caregiving that improve the patient's general health, independence, and quality of life. You can support the person you care for in maintaining their mobility, independence, and dignity as they navigate the challenges of daily living by making the environment safe, encouraging physical activity, offering assistance with mobility aids, promoting range of motion exercises, offering emotional support and encouragement.

Moving and handling/Manual handling is a broad subject which requires both theoretical and practical training, it involves training on the safe use of equipment and repositioning practices, this course will not go deeply into that.

General advice for caregivers helping a patient who has limited mobility:

- Clear clutter to create a safer environment for movement.

- Move to the individual receiving assistance's strong side.

- Always face the person you are moving or repositioning, and keep supplies and equipment close to your body.

- To bring your body down to the height where you are working, bend your knees and squat or kneel.

- Do not twist when turning; instead, pick up your feet and pivot your entire body in the direction of the motion.

- Maintain a straight back and shift your weight onto your thighs and buttocks rather than your back

NUTRITION

Helping patients with feeding is a typical way to reduce risk and relieve mealtime struggles.

Some patients can eat and drink without difficulties but they have lost dexterity in their hands, they require assistance with feeding.

General tips for assisting patients to feed

Help the patient sit at the table in a straight-backed chair that is comfortable for them to sit in and adjust the height and distance of the tabletop if they are able to get out of bed.

Before serving the food, wash and pat dry your hands.

- Give the patient a description of the dish and present it in an attractive manner.

- Use pillows to comfortably raise the patient if they are in bed.

- Remove any items from the over bed table and use a moist paper towel to clean it.

- To keep clothes and bed linens safe, use a towel or bib

- As you sit beside the patient, at eye level or lower, assist them in feeding themselves as much as you can. Don't stand while assisting the resident, you stand the risk of shoving food into their mouth and it gives the impression that you are rushing to assist them with feeding.

Some patients have difficulty in swallowing certain food and drinks, therefore their fluids and food are modified to suit their assessed needs. This difficulty in swallowing is called Dysphagia. The professionals who are specialised in assessing these needs and recommending appropriate levels of food and drinks for people are known as Speech and Language Therapist, (SALT).

Common signs of dysphagia include: coughing, choking on drinks or food, throwing up food etc.

IDDSI framework

International Dysphagia Diet Standardisation Initiative (IDDSI)

The IDDSI framework consists of a continuum of 8 levels (0 - 7), where drinks are measured from Levels 0 – 4, and foods are measured from Levels 3 – 7.

Staff must know the individual patient's food and fluid level before attempting to assist them with feeding.

FLUIDS LEVELS

Level 0 fluid is normal fluid; it means the patient can drink thin fluids without coughing

Level 1 fluid means the fluid needs to be thickened slightly by adding one scoop of a thickener to 200ml of fluid.

Level 2 fluids means the fluid should be mildly thick and you should add 2 scoops of thickener to 200ml of fluids. Level 3 fluids means the fluid should be moderately thick and you should add 3 scoops of thickener to 200ml of fluids.

Level 4 fluids mean the fluid should be extremely thick and you should add 7 scoops of thickener to the fluids.

FOOD LEVELS

Level 3 diet means Liquidised diet Level 4 diet means Pureed diet

Level 5 diet means Minced and Moist Level 6 diet means Soft and bite-sized

Level 7 diet means Regular, easy to chew diet.

It is important to know that only the Speech and Language Therapist can determine and prescribe any of the modified diets. Whenever you notice any abnormality with swallowing or drinking, notify the nurse in charge and they will do the appropriate thing.

ENVIRONMENTAL HYGIENE

To reduce the spread of infection, the environment should be kept clean, dry and tidy.

To facilitate efficient cleaning, non-essential objects should be arranged and stowed.

In a care facility, maintaining a high degree of environmental cleanliness is very important because the elderly people are susceptible to illnesses.

Even though there are cleaners whose job it is to clean the environment, the immediate patients' environment need to be kept tidy. When there is spillage, care staff should not wait for the cleaner to clean it, unless the cleaner is close by. Removing dirty pads and towels, arranging clothes in the right places, ensuring there are no equipment or furniture lying around, making sure the floors are dry, these are some of the ways the environment is kept tidy and safe for the residents.

MAINTAINING SLEEP HYGIENE

Everyone needs sleep, but patients' recovery requires it more than anyone else. From promoting the growth of new cells necessary for healing to assisting in the regulation of inflammation and providing the nervous system with rest. The importance of a good sleep cannot be overemphasized. Science-backed habits that help provide the right environment for good sleep, both during the day and before bed, are known as sleep hygiene and can make the difference between a restful and an uneasy night's sleep.

The elderly needs staff to help them promote good sleep and here are some ways through which this can be done;

It is important to know and learn what works for each patient, for some they need visual or auditory stimulation to sleep while for most people, they require a very quiet environment, for some people, they sleep with lights on while some sleep when it is pitch black.

Getting to know the residents is a very important factor. For those who have capacity to decide what they like, asking them what they want can help the staff to know their preferences.

Here are some of the general ways through which sleep can be maintained:

- TVs should be turned off two hours before bed. While it may be difficult for social media users and Kindle readers, doing this is crucial for encouraging sound sleep.
- Get rid of unwanted light.
- Make their bedding look great.
- Reduce the heat to between sixty and sixty-five degrees Fahrenheit.
- Avoid offering them stimulants in the latter part of the day

HEALTH OBSERVATION AND DOCUMENTATION.

Observation is an essential component of your job as a social care professional working in a care home to track any changes in the conditions of older persons. This makes sure that any symptoms that point to potentially dangerous new medical diseases or a decline in pre-existing ones are identified, recorded, and taken care of.

Observation is the ongoing process of monitoring any changes to an older adult's health or social welfare by combining your knowledge of them with their senses of sight, hearing, smell, and touch. Observation in a care facility is frequently divided into subjective and objective categories.

An objective observation consists of observable, quantifiable, and typically factual indicators. This involves keeping track of and documenting input/output ratios, such as any blood in the urine or stools, bruises, rashes, and allergic reactions, as well as vital signs, such as breathing, blood pressure, pulse, and temperature.

Subjective observations, on the other hand, are indications that are not quantifiable and are typically expressed verbally by the elderly person on their personal experiences, such as headaches, nausea, upset stomach, and painful muscles. The doctor or licensed nurse should be notified of these symptoms so they can be further investigated.

There are also different levels of observation which depend upon the resident's identified needs, behavior and care plans.

Level 1: General Observation

Level 2: Intermittent Observation

Level 3: Constant Observation

Level 4: Close Proximity Observation

DOCUMENTATION

For the purpose of maintaining continuity of care, accurate daily care records are crucial, especially when there are several caregivers participating or when reporting to relatives and medical experts.

Care notes ought to address things like providing personal care including skin condition, supporting with mobility, repositioning including how often and what aid was used, food intake, elimination and bowel movements including pad changes and type of faeces, and any activities they carried out.

Carer documentation guarantees that caregivers fulfill regulatory requirements and offer proof of their duty of care; it is not only a best practice but also a legal necessity.

Examples of Carers' charts and documentation

Food and drink charts are essential tools in care homes for recording residents' food consumption. They provide a visual picture of the food and drinks intake, assisting healthcare professionals in evaluating dietary practices and addressing any inadequacies. Meal logs and fluid intake diaries can be included in food and fluid charts. Both provide a comprehensive summary of people's daily food and drink intake, patterns in their intake, portion sizes, and dietary needs.

Repositioning chart is crucial to keep a record of each time a resident is moved and in what position i.e. the date, time, left, right, back. For safety reasons, repositioning is recommended at least every 6 hours for adults at risk, and every 4 hours for adults at high risk. Repositioning is a recognized strategy for preventing pressure ulcers. It involves shifting the person's posture, either on their own or with assistance (with or without the use of technology).

Elimination chart is a crucial part of a carer's documentation responsibility and has a big impact on the client's quality of life from a psychological and medical standpoint.

There must be a proper record of the pattern of bowel motions and urine output. In order to guarantee that patients are experiencing regular, soft bowel movements and sufficient urination, nurses must support patients in maintaining healthy elimination patterns and this information can best be known by Carers.

They must also recognize, report and document abnormal patterns, such as constipation, diarrhoea, incontinence, faecal impaction, haemorrhoids, and other abnormalities that may indicate underlying medical conditions.

SAFE MANAGEMENT OF WASTE

Waste is efficiently divided into the following categories, including recyclables, general waste, offensive and hygienic waste, and hazardous clinical waste.

Waste should always be handled securely and cautiously.

Never fill offensive/hygiene or clinical waste bags more than three-quarters of the way full.

When handling clinical or offensive/hygiene waste, always use the proper personal protective equipment.

Always make sure that clinical waste bags, offensive/hygiene bags, and sharps containers are securely closed, properly labeled, and stored in a secure location until they are picked up.

The guidelines recommend the following color codes: Black: domestic or general garbage

Yellow with a black stripe: Waste that is offensive or unhygienic, Orange: contagious waste

Yellow: chemical or medication-contaminated infectious waste.

Disposing of any hazardous or harmful waste with general waste is prohibited by law.

Typical offensive hygiene waste might include:
- human and animal waste (faeces)
- incontinence pads
- catheter and stoma bags
- sanitary waste
- nasal secretions and sputum
- urine.

HAND HYGIENE

One of the most crucial strategies to stop the spread of infectious organisms that lead to healthcare-associated infections (HCAIs) is to practice good hand hygiene.

Before performing hand hygiene – Expose your forearms (bare skin below the elbow), anyone wearing disposable over sleeves for religious purposes must take them off and discard them, then put on a fresh set.

Take off all bracelets and earring. It is acceptable to wear a single, simple metal finger ring, such as a wedding band, but it should be taken off (or moved higher) when practicing good hand hygiene. It is appropriate to move a religious bracelet up the forearm and secure it.

A waterproof treatment should be applied to any cuts or abrasions. Make sure your fingernails are neat and short, and refrain from wearing artificial nails or nail products.

Use water and non-antimicrobial liquid soap to wash your hands if:

– Hands are obviously filthy or unclean when tending to individuals who have vomiting or diarrheal diseases.

– Taking care of a patient who has a spore-forming bacterium, such Clostridium difficile, or a known or suspected gastrointestinal infection, like norovirus.

5 moments of hand hygiene:
- before touching a patient.
- before clean or aseptic procedures.
- after body fluid exposure risk
- after touching a patient; and
- after touching a patient's immediate surroundings.

Always perform hand hygiene before putting on and after removing gloves.

PERSONAL PROTECTIVE EQUIPMENT (PPE)

PPE is equipment worn to minimize exposure to a variety of hazards.

Personal Protective Equipment (PPE) is used for several reasons including:

- To protect staff from blood, body fluid and microbiological contamination.
- To reduce the risk of cross infection to other individuals and the patients care environment.
- Reduces the risk of HealthCare Associated Infections (HCAIs).

PPE that is reusable, such as goggles, face shields, and visors, needs to be decontaminated according to the manufacturer's instructions after every use.

PPE are single-use only unless the manufacturer specifies otherwise.

PPE need to be changed immediately after each patient and/or after completing a procedure or task.

PPE are to be disposed of into the appropriate waste stream after usage, such as household waste, offensive (non-infectious), or clinical waste.

PPE to be disposed of if damaged or contaminated.

Examples of PPE include:
- Gloves Aprons
- full-face visors
- Fluid resistant surgical face masks

SAFE MANAGEMENT OF LINEN

When handling clean linen, hands need to be kept clean. The linen ought to be clean, functional, and free of stains or damage. Don't keep clean clothes and linens in the laundry room. When not in use for other purposes, a clean dedicated room or cabinet should be utilized to store clean linens.

Clean linen is any linen that is washed and ready for usage.

Used (soiled and fouled) linen is any linen that has been used, irrespective of state, which on occasion may be contaminated by blood or body fluids.

Infectious linen is any linen that has been used by a patient who is suspected or confirmed to be infectious.

Do not rinse, shake or sort linen on removal from beds/trolleys

Do not place used linen on the floor or any other surfaces e.g. a locker/table top

Do not re-handle used linen once bagged

Do not overfill laundry receptacles (not more than 2/3 full); Do not place inappropriate items in the laundry receptacle e.g. used equipment/needles

Make sure there is a laundry basket near the point of usage so that linens can be deposited right away.

Instead of sorting, infectious linen should be rolled up and sealed in a water-soluble bag (an impermeable bag with soluble seams or an entirely water-soluble "alginate" bag).

This is usually a red bag. This bag should then be placed in an impermeable bag as soon as the patient is taken out of bed and fastened before being removed from a clinical area.

As soon as the linen is taken off the bed or before departing a clinical department, it should be sealed in an impermeable bag.

BUILDING RESILIENCE AS A CARER

Diving into the world of caregiver, where every day is a wild roller coaster ride of challenges, from juggling emotions to superhero-like feats of strength and empathy. In the UK alone, over 6.5 million unsung heroes step up to care for loved ones, friends, or neighbors facing health challenges, old age, or disabilities. Keeping these caregivers mentally strong and happy is crucial for both their well-being and the quality of care they dish out. Let's crack open the treasure chest of strategies to boost their resilience and sprinkle some glitter on their mental health!

Resilience, the superpower to bounce back from life's curve balls, is like a rubber band snapping back into shape after being stretched. It's that mental muscle we flex during tough times. On the flip side, psychological well-being is like a rainbow of feels about oneself and life, covering everything from self-love to kicking life goals and having rock-solid relationships.

For caregivers, resilience and well-being are the secret sauces that keep them going strong in the care giving marathon. To prevent burnout and keep mental health in top gear, these caregiver warriors need to tackle stress head-on by spotting the usual suspects: exhaustion, lack of resources, dealing with care-receiver conflicts, social isolation, and lack of recognition for the important work they do. It's like a game of whack-a-mole, but with self-care strategies as the mighty hammer!

- **Building Resilience through Social Support**

    Social support is a linchpin for resilience-building. Carers need avenues to share experiences, obtain advice, and feel understood within a community. Initiatives such as carer support groups, whether online or in-person, offer a forum for exchange and solidarity. Additionally, respite care services provide the opportunity for carers to take necessary breaks, recognizing that rest is fundamental for resilience.

- **Enhancing Psychological Well-being with Self-care**

    Just as an aircraft safety briefing advises individuals to put on their oxygen masks before helping others, carers must tend to their own needs first to maintain their psychological well-being. Self-care practices such as maintaining a healthy diet, engaging in physical activity, and pursuing hobbies can significantly buffer the stress of care giving. These activities offer the dual purpose of enhancing personal health and serving as a recharge, equipping carers with more energy to care for others.

- **Developing Emotional Intelligence**

    Another vital component in building resilience is emotional intelligence—the ability to recognize, understand, control, and harness emotions. Carers with high emotional intelligence can better comprehend the emotional states of themselves and their care recipients, allowing them to manage challenging situations with greater ease. Learning techniques such as mindfulness and reflective practice can assist in developing emotional intelligence, thus fortifying their psychological resilience.

♦ **Education And Skills Training**

Empowering carers with the knowledge and skills to perform their roles effectively is critical. Education and training not only heighten the quality of care provided but also build confidence and competence, which enhances well being. From practical care giving skills to understanding the particular health conditions of the residents/care recipients, this education serves as a critical foundation for resilience.

♦ **Accessing Professional Help**

Sometimes the help needed is more than what self-help and community organizations can provide. Professional counselling or therapy can play a critical role in helping caregivers manage grief, deal with complex emotions, and create coping mechanisms for persistent challenges. Professionals can also help create a customized resilience-building plan that takes into account each caregiver's particular situation.

♦ **Advocacy and Policy Support**

To enhance the support system for caregivers, policymakers must collaborate to provide resources and acknowledgment. This involves advocating for funding, improved employment rights, and integrating caregiver needs into healthcare planning.

Prioritizing caregivers' well-being in policies emphasizes the significance of their role, ultimately enhancing their mental health.

IN CLOSING

The idea behind developing a caregiver manual is based on a fundamental truth: caregiving is a combination of science and art. This manual goes beyond being a mere guide; it represents a dedication to maintaining the dignity and respect of caregivers, benefiting both caregivers and the organizations supporting them. It acts as a vital resource for individuals and groups, guiding caregivers on their noble journey towards excellence and compassionate service.

Improving the mental well-being and resilience of caregivers necessitates a holistic approach that includes systemic, communal, and individual components. As members of society, it is our shared duty to safeguard the welfare of those devoted to caregiving. Through establishing a strong support network, promoting education, advocating for self-care practices, and supporting policies, we can strengthen the mental and emotional resilience of caregivers while acknowledging their priceless contributions. By enriching the lives of caregivers, we, as a society, ensure a more resilient and compassionate care system for all.

Milton Keynes UK
Ingram Content Group UK Ltd.
UKHW050300130824
446846UK00004B/23